Kali The Mother

Owing to the antiquity and rarity of this book, certain pages are regrettably absent, and readability is compromised due to the blurring of the original text. If you possess any insights regarding the availability of these missing sections, kindly inform us. Your assistance is crucial in ensuring the completion of this significant work for the benefit of future generations.

Kali The Mother

BY

THE SISTER NIVEDITA

GYAN

Published by

GYAN

Gyan Publishing House
5, Ansari Road
Daryaganj, New Delhi-110002
Phone: 011-47034999, 9811692060
E-mail: books@gyanbooks.com

Distribution Network
gyanbooks.com
India, USA, Canada, UK, Australia

ISBN: 978-81-212-0957-1 (HB)
First Published, 1900

2nd Impression 2024

Printed at: Gyan Press, Delhi.

KALI THE MOTHER
Author: SISTER NIVEDITA

Kali the Mother

To

Vireshwar—

Lord of heroes.

Kali The Mother

By
The Sister NIVEDITA
Of the Order of Ramakrishna
Calcutta, India.

Contents

Concerning Symbols.

OUR daily life creates our symbol of God. No two ever cover quite the same conception.

It is so with that symbolism which we know as language. The simple daily needs of mankind, seem, the world over, to be one. We look, therefore, for words that correspond in every land.

Yet we know how the tongue of each people expresses some one group of ideas with especial clearness, and ignores others altogether. Never do we find an identical strength and weakness repeated: and always if we go deep enough, we can discover in the circumstances and habits of a country, a cause for its specific difference of thought or of expression.

In the North we speak of a certain hour as "twilight," implying a space of time between the day and night. In India, the same moments receive the name of "time of union," since there is no period of half-light,—the hours of sun and darkness seeming to touch each other in a point.

The illustration can be carried further. In the word *gloaming* lies for us a wealth of associations,—the throbbing of the falling dusk, the tenderness of home-coming, the last sleepy laughter of children. The same emotional note is struck in Indian languages by the expression *at the hour of cowdust.*

How graphic is the difference! Yonder, beyond the grass, the cow-girl leads her cattle home to the village for the night. Their feet as they go strike the dust from the sun-baked path into a cloud behind them. The herd-girl herself looms large across the pasture—all things grow quickly dim, as if the air were filled with rising dust.

That word *cowdust,* indeed, strikes a whole vein of expression peculiar to this Eastern land. Everything about the cow has been observed and loved and named. As much water as will lie in the hole once made by its hoof is a well known measure amongst the Aryan folk!

It is unnecessary to argue further

that while the facts of nature determine the main developments of speech, yet every language and group of languages differs from every other as the characters of individuals and of nations.

Something of the same sort is true of religious symbols. Short of perfect realization, we must see the Eternal Light through a mask imposed by our own thought. To no two of us, probably, is the mask quite in the same place, and some reach, by their own growth, diverging points so distant from the common centre that they mark the extreme limits hitherto achieved of those great areas known as the Christian, or the Buddhist, or the this-that-or-the-other consciousness.

To do this, or even to carry a whole race to a new rallying-place round a standard planted on the old frontier is the peculiar mission of religious genius.

So Jesus swept down in His might on the old Jewish entrenchments of justice—righteousness—

and carried the banner off bodily to that outpost of love and mercy which struggling souls had reached, indeed, before Him, but which none had yet been strong enough to make the very heart and focus of vitality.

And so every one of us, simply by thinking his own thought, and living his own life to the full, may be answering his brother's cry for God in ways beyond the dreaming of the world. Are Catholic possibilities not richer for the life of Manning, or Protestant for Frances Ridley Havergal?

These things being true, the imagery of all men has its significance for us. The mask is created by our own thought directly, and indirectly through the reaction of custom upon thought. Like all veils, it brings at once vision and the limiting of vision. Only by realising the full sense of every symbol can we know the whole thought of Humanity about God.

But down with all masks!

The Uncreated Flame itself we

long for, without symbol or veil or barrier. If we cannot see God and live,—let us then die—what is there to fear? Consume us in primal fire, dissolve us into living ocean, but interpose nothing, no, nor the shadow of anything, between the soul and the divine draught for which it thirsts!

True. Yet for each of us there is a chosen way. We ourselves may still be seeking it, where and when still hidden from our eyes. But deep in our hearts is rooted the assurance that the moment will yet come, the secret signal be exchanged, the mystic name will fall upon our ears, and somewhere, somewhen, somehow, our feet shall pass within the gates of Peace, we shall enter on the road that ends only with the Beatific Vision.

Till then, well says the old Hindu poet of the folk-song to himself:—

"Tulsi, coming into this world,
Seek thou to live with all—
For who knows where or in what guise,
The Lord Himself may come to thee?"

Our daily life creates our symbol of God.

To the Arab of the desert, with his patriarchal customs, the father of the family,—just and calm in his judgments, protector of his kindred, loving to those who played about his knees as babes,—may well stand as the type of all in which men feel security.

Naturally, then, it was the Semitic mind that flashed across the dim communing of the soul with the Eternal, the rapturous illumination of the great word "Father."

God our father,—bound even to the most erring of His children by a kinship that misdoing cannot break (for if the human tie be indissoluble, shall the divine be less so?); father, —by a tie so intimate that to this day the stalwart Afghan, prostrating in the mosque, says "Thee" and "Thou" to the God of Hosts, as might an infant on its father's knee!

In the Aryan home, woman stands supreme. As wife in the West,—lady and queen of her husband—as mother in the East,—a goddess throned in her son's worship,—she is the bringer of sanctity and peace.

Profound depths stir within us, in presence of the intensely Christian conception of God—a child in His mother's arms. This ideal of the heart of a woman—pierced by its seven sorrows, on fire with love, mother beside the cradle, worshipper beneath the cross, and glorified in great humility,—has been one of the richest gifts of the Catholic Church to humanity.

Peerless in its own way is the womanhood of Rossetti's sonnet :—

> "This is that blessed Mary, pre-elect
> God's Virgin. Gone is a great while, and she
> Dwelt young in Nazareth of Galilee . .
> Unto God's will she brought devout respect,—
> Profound simplicity of intellect,
> And supreme patience . . . . . .
> Thus held she through her girlhood,
> As it were an angel-watered lily,
> That near God grows, and is quiet."

Jesus Himself—to those who kneel before no Madonna in the Vatican—sounds this note of the eternal feminine. "Come unto me, all ye that labour, and are heavy laden, and I will refresh you. Take my yoke upon you, and learn of me, for I am meek and lowly of heart, and ye shall find rest unto your souls." Is it not a woman's cry?

Nay, He is conscious of this element in His own nature. Once at least He speaks of it. In that sublime moment when He, the young Leader of the armies of the future, stands on the sunlit mountains, and looking down upon the city of His race sees the dark shadow of destiny wrapping it about, in that moment when the Patriot forgets, in a sob of human anguish, that He is Master and Redeemer, in that moment He becomes all motherhood. "O Jerusalem! Jerusalem! Thou that killest the prophets, and stonest them that are sent unto thee,—how often would I have gathered thy children together, like as a hen gathereth her chickens under her wings, and ye would not!"

The soul that worships becomes always a little child: the soul that becomes a child finds God oftenest as mother. In a meditation before the Blessed Sacrament, some pen has written the exquisite assurance: "My child, you need not know much in order to please Me. Only love Me dearly. Speak to me, as you would talk to your mother, if she had taken you in her arms."

But it is in India that this thought of the mother has been realised in its completeness. In that country where the image of Kali is one of the most popular symbols of deity, it is quite customary to speak of God, as "She," and the direct address then offered is simply "Mother."

But under what strange guise! In the West, art and poetry have been exhausted to associate all that is tender and precious with this thought of woman-worship. The mother plays with the little One, or caresses or nurses Him. Sometimes she even makes her arm a throne, whereon He sits to bless the world.

In the East, the accepted symbol is of a woman nude, with flowing hair, so dark a blue that she seems in colour to be black, four-handed—two hands in the act of blessing, and two holding a knife and bleeding head respectively,—garlanded with skulls, and dancing, with protruding tongue, on the prostrate figure of a man all white with ashes.

A terrible, an extraordinary figure ! Those who call it horrible may well be forgiven. They pass only through the outer court of the temple. They are not arrived where the Mother's voice can reach them. This, in its own way is well.

Yet, this image, so fearful to the Western mind, is perhaps dearer than any other to the heart of India. It is not, indeed, the only form in which the Divine Energy presents Herself to Her worshippers. To the Sikh, She is absorbed, embodied in his sword ; all women, especially as children, are Her incarnations ; glorious Sita carries the great reality to many.

But Kali comes closer to us than these. Others we admire; others we love; to Her we belong. Whether we know it or not, we are Her children, playing round Her knees. Life is but a game of hide-and-seek with Her, and if, in its course, we chance to touch Her feet, who can measure the shock of the divine energy that enters into us? Who can utter the rapture of our cry of "Mother?"

The Vision of Siva.

Dark Mother! Always gliding near with soft feet,
Have none chanted for Thee a chant of fullest welcome?

Walt Whitman.

IT may have been that the forefathers saw it in the mountains. Or it may have been elsewhere. Somewhere it came to the Hindu mind that the beauty of snowpeaks and moonlight, and standing water, was different from all other loveliness of colour and profusion and many-channelled scene.

It was as though Nature, the great Mother, were clothed in raiment of green, broidered with birds and flowers and fruits, and veiled in blue, adorned with many jewels, and yet as if, amidst all the restless pomp and clamour of her glory, would shine through now and then, a hint of something different. Something white and austere and pure ; something compelling quiet ; something silent and passionless, and eternally alone. Even the beauty of the world, then, suggested a twofold essence. Wherever the Hindu looked, he found this duality repeated,—light and shadow, attraction and repulsion, microcosm and macrocosm, cause and effect. Nay, he looked into human life itself, and he found humanity as man and woman, soul and body.

Here was a clue. On the plane of symbolism, the soul of things somehow became associated with the manly form, and the manifested energy (Nature, as we call it) with that of woman and motherhood. In this conception will be noted the deliberate statement that God and Nature are necessary to each other as the complementary manifestations of One, just as we find in the male and the female together, Humanity. That is to say, Nature itself is God, as truly as Nature's soul. "Are God and Nature then at strife?" cries, not only a great poet, but the whole heart of our western religion to-day. And far back from out of the dim centuries comes the hushed whisper of the Indian sages—"Look closer, brother! they are not even two, but one!" Under this aspect, the One Existence is known as Purush and Prakriti, Soul and Energy.

The highest representation of the Divine is always human. The shadow of a great rock in a weary land is a beautiful presentment of some imaginary qualities of God, but not for one moment does it delude the mind into the belief that here at last it has the thing itself. So with the Light and the Door, the Mountain and the Shield. These were not images that could take captive both brain and heart, firing a man to die in their defence. Very different was it with those other pictures, the Good Shepherd, the Eternal Father !

Here a strange mental confusion is imminent. The mystery behind all form is at last named in a formula so convincing, so appealing, so satisfying, that distinction ceases ; we forget that even this is not final, that beyond the expression, and apart from it, lies the whole immensity.

Hinduism has avoided this danger of fixedness in a very curious way. Of all the peoples of the earth, it might be claimed that Hindus are apparently the most, and at heart the least, idolatrous. For the application of their symbols is many-centred, like the fire in opals.

This Purush and Prakriti utters a great principle. The relation of God to Nature is one demonstration of it. The soul and experience offer us another. The dynamo and the force that charges it would be a third.

This last illustration deserves a moment's attention. Everywhere we see the phenomenon of one waiting to be touched by another, in order to manifest power and activity. The two are known in India as Siva and Sakti. As the knight waits for the sight of his own lady, powerless without the inspiration of her touch, as the disciple waits for the master, and finds in him at last the meaning of all his life before, so the soul lies inert, passive, unstirred by the external, till the great moment comes, and it looks up at the shock of some divine catastrophe, to know in a flash that the whole of the without,—the whole of life, and time, and nature, and experience—like the within, is also God.

It is the beatific vision, says the West: it is realisation of the Self, here and now, declares the East.

Of such a moment is the Kali image symbol—the soul opening its eyes upon the world and seeing God.

We have seen that anthropomorphic representation of the Divine is absolutely necessary to human nature. But to learn the manner and method of that expression, we must know the whole heart and feeling of a people. To us, ideal manhood includes the king, the master, and the father. He must be supreme. He goes forth before His armies as general and sovereign. He counts the very hairs of His children's heads. He avenges their wrongs, and He protects from pestilence. He owns the vineyard of the world, and Himself prunes and cares for the chosen vine. Perfect in love, perfect in administration, perfect in power: ideal householder, ideal judge, ideal ruler. Such is the anthropomorphism of the West.

How strangely different is that of India! There, life has one test, one standard, and one alone. Does a man know God or not? That is all. No question of fruits, no question of activity, no question of happiness. Only—has the soul set out on the quest of realisation?

How literally this is the one passion we may see in popular drama. There, the romantic motive is of no account. That Jack should have his Joan (or not have her) is a mere incident, passed over with no superfluous words, at the beginning of things. But we sit for hours absorbed, enthralled, to know—when shall these men attain to God? Or even, when shall they discover that nothing but God is worth the having?

And of this stage of developement, renunciation is accepted as the outward sign. For in that moment when the red rose of the love of God springs and blossoms in a man's heart,—so that he cries out: "Like as the hart panteth after the waterbrooks, *so* longeth my soul after Thee O God!"—in that moment, as Asia knows well, everything else falls away from him. All the manifold satisfactions of the flesh become a burden. Home and kindred and intercourse with the world are a bondage. Food and sleep and the necessities of the physical life seem indifferent or intolerable. And so it comes that the Great God of the Hindu imagination is a beggar. Covered with the ashes of His sacrificial fire, so that He is white like snow, His hair growing untended in huge masses, oblivious of cold or heat, silent, remote from men, He sits absorbed in eternal meditation.

Those human eyes of His are half closed. Though worlds are uttered and destroyed with every breath, it is nothing to Him. All comes and goes before Him like a dream. Such is the meaning of the curious unrealism of the image.

But one faculty is all activity. Within it has been indrawn all the force of all the senses. Upright in the middle of the forehead looks forth the third eye, the eye of inner vision. It is natural then, that Siva the Great God, set forth as ideal manhood, should be known amongst other names as the Wondrous-Eyed.

He is the Refuge of Animals. About His neck have wound the serpents, whom none else would receive.

Never did he turn any away. The mad and the eccentric, the crazed, and the queer, and the half-witted amongst men—for all these there is room with Siva. His love will embrace even the demoniac.

He accepts that which all else reject. All the pain and evil of the Universe He took as His share, to save the world, when He drank the poison of things, and made His throat blue for ever.

He possesses so little! Only the old bull on which he rides, and the tiger-skin of meditation, and a string or two of praying beads—no more.

And, last of all, He is so easily pleased! Could any trait be so exquisite as this? Only pure water and a few grains of rice, and a green leaf or two may be offered to Him daily, for the Great God in matters of this world is very very simple, and sets no store by things for which we struggle and lie and slay our fellow men. Such is the picture that springs to the Indian mind, as representing the Soul of the Universe—Siva, the All-Merciful, the Destroyer of Ignorance, the Great God. Such is the form in which are uttered finally those first faint suggestions of the light of Himalayan snow peaks and the new moon shining on still waters. Perfect renunciation, perfect withdrawnness, perfect absorption in eternity,—these things alone are worthy to be told concerning Him Who is "the Sweetest of the Sweet, the most Terrible of the Terrible, the Lord of Heroes, and the Wondrous-Eyed."

Listen to the prayer that rises to Him daily from many a worshipper, through the length and breadth of India :—

" From the Unreal lead us to the Real,
From Darkness lead us unto Light,
From Death lead us to Immortality.
Reach us through and through ourself,
And evermore protect us,—
O Thou Terrible !—from ignorance,
By Thy sweet compassionate face."

Such is Siva—ideal of Manhood, embodiment of Godhead.

As the Purush, or Soul, He is Consort and Spouse of Maya, Nature, the fleeting diversity of sense. It is in this relation that we find Him beneath the feet of Kali. His recumbent posture signifies inertness, the Soul untouched and indifferent to the external. Kali has been executing a wild dance of carnage. On all sides She has left evidences of Her reign of terror. The garland of skulls is round her neck ; still in Her hands She holds the bloody weapon and a freshly-severed head. Suddenly She has stepped unwittingly on the body of Her Husband. Her foot is on His breast. He has looked up, awakened by that touch, and They are gazing into each other's eyes. Her right hands are raised in involuntary blessing, and Her tongue makes an exaggerated gesture of shyness and surprise, once common to Indian women of the villages.

And He, what does He see? To Him, She is all beauty--this woman nude and terrible and black, who tells the name of God on the skulls of the dead, who creates the blood-shed on which demons fatten, who slays rejoicing and repents not, and blesses Him only that lies crushed beneath Her feet.

Her mass of black hair flows behind Her like the wind, or like time, "the drift and passage of things." But to the great third eye even time is one, and that one, God. She is blue almost to blackness, like a mighty shadow, and bare like the dread realities of life and death. But for Him there is no shadow. Deep into the heart of that Most Terrible, He looks unshrinking, and in the ecstasy of recognition He calls Her *Mother*. So shall ever be the union of the soul with God.

Do we understand what the background is from which such a thought as this could spring? For the Kali-image is not so much a picture of the deity, as the utterance of the secret of our own lives.

The soul in realisation beholds the mother—how? The picture of green lawns and smiling skies, and flowers steeped in sunshine, cannot deceive the All-Knower. Under the apparent loveliness, He sees life preying on life, the rivers breaking down the mountains, the comet poised in mid-space to strike. Around him rises up the wail of all the creatures, the moan of pain, and the sob of greed, and the pitiful cry of little things in fear. Irresponsible, without mercy, seems the spirit of time—deaf to the woes of man, or answering them only with a peal of laughter.

Such is the world as the Hindu mind is predisposed to see it. "Verily," says the heart wearily, "Death is greater than Life, yea and better!"

Not so the supreme soul in its hour of vision! No coward's sigh of exhaustion, no selfish prayer for mercy, no idle resignation there! Bend low, and you shall hear the answer that India makes to the Eternal Motherhood, through all her ages of torture and despair. Listen well, for the voice is low that speaks, and the crash of ruin mighty:—

"Though Thou slay me, *yet* will I trust in Thee!" After all, has anyone of us found God in any other form than in this—the Vision of Siva? Have not the great intuitions of our life all come to us in moments when the cup was bitterest? Has it not always been with sobs of desolation that we have seen the Absolute triumphant in Love?

Behold we also, O Mother, are Thy children! Though Thou Slay us, yet will we trust in Thee!

. . . . . .

The hour is gone, and the vision is passed away, the vision of the greatest symbol, perhaps, that man has ever imagined for himself. The hour is past, and we are back amongst the mountains in the early ages.

There is a gathering of the tribes for a Vedic sacrifice. Yonder, the bull majestically paces towards us, laden with wood for the sacrificial fire.

Now it is lighted, and from the central mass rises the blue-throated flame, while round the edge, leaving the fuel black and charred, curl those greedy red tongues of fire, to each of which the wise men give its separate name—the Black, the Terrible, and so on. The priests chant texts, and the people wait upon the worship. And we see faces-in-the-fire of the time to be, when the eyes of the poet shall rest upon the sacrifice, and shall fashion therefrom this mighty vision of God and nature, the soul and life.

For scholars say that Siva is but the fire of Vedic rites personified. He is the wood borne upon the bull, and the flame which is white, with a patch of blue colour at the throat.

As for Kali, She, it is claimed, was one of His powers, one of the red licking flames, which char and blacken the wood that is not consumed. In token of which we see to this day Her protruding tongue.

Two Saints of Kali.

GREATNESS is but another word for interpretation. We feel the very presence of some persons as if it were the translation of poems from a foreign tongue. Every profound truth waits for the life that shall be all its voice, and when that is found it comes within the reach of multitudes to whom it would have remained inaccessible.

But we cannot find truth in a word, unless it is illumined by our own experience. That statement which we have lived but have not spoken, even to ourselves, when uttered by another's lips, we hail as revelation. And that alone. What we have ourselves once said seems commonplace, and that which is too far above we do not understand.

So it happens that the interpreter, the poet, must be for ever telling to the world those things of which it has already won heart-knowledge. This is the sign that we demand always from the messenger—that he speak of a common memory. And to him who does this we listen gladly, believing that life will yet bring the significance of those words of his that do not, for the nonce, explain themselves to us.

Highest of all the poets stands the saint. His task is not to take the brilliant patches of love, and sorrow and heroism, and fit them into jewelled settings for the admiration of the many. He takes the whole of life, all the grey, sombre stuff of which it is chiefly made, and the blackest and the brightest with this, and throws on the whole a new light, till even in the eyes of those who suffer it, life is made beautiful. The dramatist deals only with dramatic motives, but to him all is dramatic. The petty needs of childhood are no less related to the World-Heart than the passion by which Othello slays Desdemona.

But that new tune to which he sets the old song of living has to be caught in snatches from the people, a note here and a cadence there. The mother crooning her babe to rest, or wailing beside it in its last long sleep; the man panting for his adversary, or finding himself inadequate to the protection of those he loves; the peasant guiding the plough with patient strength, the child-folk playing in the sunlight, all these have whispered him in the ear, and taught him the whole of their mystic lore.

It is not then the voice of the prophet, but the great heart of the vulgar, that brings a new religious intuition to the birth. All that violence and gesticulation that repel us, are but the dim experimental utterance of an impulse not yet fully conscious of itself.

It is when the idea has been elaborated in this way by the imagination and conscience of the myriads, that there arises a man who seems to embody it in his own person. And he is hailed as Master and Teacher by all, because he interprets their own lives, and speaks the words that already they were struggling to express. He is the crest of the wave, but all these are the wave itself.

Born thus of his nation's life, and speaking straight to its heart was

Ram Prasad, the great Bengali poet of the Motherhood of God. Not a century has passed since a crowd stood with him by the Ganges-side, listening to his recital of his own finest work. As he pronounced the last words the old man exclaimed, "It is achieved," and on the moment died. It was not death. It was translation. And the people feel that it happened yesterday.

He had begun life as a book-keeper, and no doubt tried, when he remembered them, to perform his duties faithfully. But when at the end of a week his employer called for his books, he found on the first page a sonnet beginning—"Mother! make me thine accountant. I shall never prove defaulter," and verses scribbled all over the accounts. One cry, "Mother! Mother!" rang through every line, and as the Hindu does not live who cannot understand a religious freak, his genius was recognised at once. A small pension was settled on him, and he was set free from wage earning for the rest of his life.

The result is a collection of folk-songs, full of the sentiment of Kali-worship, left to the memories of his people. Many it is to be feared, remain about the villages of Bengal, unrecorded to this day. But they are so integral a part of the life that there is good reason to trust that they will never be lost.

In after days, Ram Prasad became famous. Drifting down the Ganges one summer day, his little boat encountered the royal barge of Surajah Dowlah, the brilliant young governor of Bengal, and he was ordered to come on board and sing. The poet tuned his vina, and racked his brain for songs in the grand old classic style, fine enough to suit the presence. But the Mohammedan would have none of them—"Sing me your own songs—About the Mother!" he commanded graciously, and his subject was only too glad to obey.

No flattery could touch a nature so unapproachable in its simplicity. For in these writings we have perhaps alone in literature, the spectacle of a great poet, whose genius is spent in realising the emotions of a child. William Blake, in our own poetry, strikes the note that is nearest his, and Blake is by no means his peer.

Robert Burns in his splendid indifference to rank, and Whitman in his glorification of common things, have points of kinship with him. But to such a radiant white-heat of child-likeness, it would be impossible to find a perfect counterpart. His years do nothing to spoil this quality. They only serve to give him self-confidence and poise. Like a child he is now grave, now gay, sometimes petulant, sometimes despairing. But in the child all this is purposeless: in Ram Prasad there is a deep intensity of purpose. Every sentence he has uttered is designed to sing the glory of his Mother.

For all his simplicity, however, our author is not to be understood without an effort. Nor need this surprise us. It takes the whole history of Rome and Florence to make the Divina Commedia comprehensible. In fact we can never understand any poet without some knowledge of the culture that produced him, and what is true of Dante may be expected to prove still more applicable to one who is removed from us by oceans and continents, as well as by the complex civilising centuries.

Indeed it may be questioned whether the apparent artlessness of Oriental expression is not always somewhat misleading. Into four lines of landscape, we are told, the Chino-Japanese can slip the whole theory of his national existence, without ever a European suspecting double purpose; and much the same is the case with the Hindu. A wealth of such associations goes for instance to the appreciation of the great line describing the mountain-forests against the snow, —"They make eternal sati on the body of Mahadev."

What is said of the Japanese artist is pre-eminently true of Ram Prasad, only it is in the broken toys and April shower and sunshine of a child's moods that he hides the mysteries of the universe.

Apart from his passion of devotion to the Divine Motherhood, there is a whole conception of life in his mind which is unfamiliar to us. The East takes such an utterance as "the pure in heart shall *see* God" very literally. It places the ideal existence, not in salvation—or in the condition of being delivered from sinfulness—but in this very power of direct perception of the Divine.

It seems to the Asiatic mind that the body is an actual hindrance to cognition. It is not that meaning is conveyed by language, but that mind is drawn near to mind. In unskilled speech, words may serve only to conceal thought, but in the most skilled they cannot do more than suggest it. Nerves do not create suffering, for the joy and sorrow that we share in imagination can be far keener than our own. And so this convention, of sight—sound—touch—taste—smell, under which we become aware of the not-myself, is merely a formula which deadens the Real for us till we are strong enough to bear it ; and we must stay in the body, or return to it, till we have in some way mastered these conditions.

When limitation is broken, however, when every dim stratum and substratum of our being has become conscious, and the whole consciousness is gathered up into the single tremendous act of knowledge,—not the conventionalised, formulated awareness of the senses, but direct absolute knowledge,—what is it claimed that we perceive? That which came before as many, as seeing and hearing and the rest, is known now to be One, and that One—God.

And so it happens that the great goal of Eastern religion is known as Mukti or Nirvana, or Freedom. The man in whom this perception is perfected is liberated from conditions—he may subject himself to them at will, but he is not bound by them. He has left the sleep of ignorance behind him, and is for ever awake. Says Ram Prasad :—

" From the land where there is no night
    Has come One unto me.
And night and day are now nothing to me,
Ritual-worship has become for ever barren.

My sleep is broken. Shall I sleep any
    more?
Call it what you will—I am awake—
Hush! I have given back sleep unto Him
    whose it was.
Sleep have I put to sleep for ever.

The music has entered the instrument,
And of that mode I have learnt a song.
Ah! that music is playing ever before
    me,
For concentration is the great teacher
    thereof.
Prasad speaks—Understand, O Soul, these
    words of Wisdom."

But the great burden of his verses is the Mother. And in calling upon Her he becomes the ideal child. It is curious to reflect how a century and a half ago, almost a hundred years before the birth of childhood into European art, a great Indian singer and saint should have been deep in observation of the little ones—studying them, and sharing every feeling, almost without knowing it himself.

Once, indeed, he seems to justify himself—

"Whom else should I cry to, Mother?
The baby cries for its mother alone—
And I am not the son of such
That I should call any woman my mother!

Tho' the mother beat him,
The child cries 'Mother, O Mother!'
And clings still tighter to her garment.

True I cannot see Thee,
Yet am I not a lost child!
I still cry 'Mother, Mother!'"

But indignant pride gives way to secret despair, mingled with an angry impatience. God must be dead—no living mother could so long resist a baby's cries. He will hold a funeral in effigy, and retire from the world for ever.

"Mind, stop calling 'Mother, Mother!'
Don't you know She is dead?—
Else why should She not come?

I am going to the banks of the Ganges,
To burn the grass image of my Mother,
And then I'll go and live in Benares."

When the question of his going

on pilgrimage, however, is seriously mooted, he makes a reply of wonderful beauty and profundity. Naughty as he is, he does not want to go, and is willing to support himself with reasons. Doubt leads to doubt and a frown culminates in a supreme defiance :—

"Why should I go to Benares?
My Mother's lotus-feet
Are millions and millions
Of holy places.

The books say, man dying in Benares
Attains Nirvana.
I believe it. Siva has said it.
But the root of all is devotion
And freedom is her slave.
What good is there even in Nirvana?
Mixing water with water——!
See I do not care to *become* sugar,
I want to *eat* sugar!"

What a flash is in those last two lines! The shrewd mother-wit of a peasant joins with the insight of a great poet, not only to express the finest of fine emotions—the joy of being the inferior, but to hint in the same words, at the secret of existence.

Quaint beyond quaintness is the

song of the kite-flying. To the child mind it is quite natural that its mother should play with its toys. All mothers do so. And now Kali becomes the playmate. Her toy is the Indian kite, of which the string is covered with powdered glass that it may cut through others. But the boy forgets his game, so completely is it She that fascinates him. He breaks away and looks on with grave joy at Her, while his lips involuntarily frame a song. It is the game of life, that is played before him; the kite released is the soul, gone to freedom; and still the Mother laughs and plays on, as if She knew not that all these were shadows:—

"In the market place of this world,
The Mother sits flying Her kite.
In a hundred thousand,
She cuts the string of one or two.
And when the kite soars up into the
Infinite
Oh how She laughs and claps her hands!"

Again he is making a mystery out of nothing, playing hide and seek, as babies love to do.

"The name of Her whom I call my Mother, shall I tell that secret to the world?" he says (lit. "Shall I break the pot before the market?") "Even then who knows Her? Lo, the six philosophies were not able to find out Kali!"

That is almost the only simile in which he ceases to be a child, when he adjures himself to "Dive deep, O soul, taking the name of Kali!" into that ocean of beauty from which he is to bring up the lustrous pearl.

So much then for the art-form in which this worship of tender appeal has been enshrined. To the Hindu mind the poet's familiarity with his Mother makes him not only dear and great, but infinitely devout. It proves, as did the repartee of S. Theresa, that God is more real to him than the objects and persons that we see about us daily. Is it not true that a soul so close to the Divine might well have been that child who was taken on Christ's knee when He said:—"Of such is the kingdom of heaven."

It is not as the interpreter of man's love to God, but as the great Incarnation of the spirit of the Mother towards Her children, that we pass on and kneel at the feet of Ramakrishna Paramahamsa.

Here is one who has but lately gone out from amongst us. Less than twenty years ago he was teaching in the Temple-Garden of Dukineshwar, near Calcutta. And so large loomed the Divine through him, that many of those who knew and loved him then, speak his name to this day with bated breath, calling him, "Our Lord."

For in the case of Ramakrishna, innumerable prayers and unheard-of austerities had culminated in a realisation so profound that there was scarcely a memory of selfhood left. The man who lived and moved before his disciples was a mere shell, that could not fail to act as the indwelling motherhood willed. He never used, it is said, the expression "I" and "mine," preferring "He who dwells here" (indicating His own heart), or usually "My holy Mother."

That his original phyisque must have been extraordinary, we can infer, since it stood the strain under which his religious yearning hurried it, for fifty-three years. But far more wonderful was the complexity and many sidedness of character and of development, that made him feel the perplexities of every heart as if they were his own. His was, probably, the one really universal mind of modern times. Yet the whole was wrought to such a unity that the peace of it fills to this day the little chamber where he dwelt, and abides like a mighty presence under the great tree of meditation. That little room, how poor, even to meanness, it looked when I last saw it!

It was night, and a tiny lamp—a cup of oil with a floating wick—illumined the exquisite purity of bed-linen and the fresh flowers placed by faithful hands before the Master's picture. The lamp was lifted, and the long shadows seemed to come down, from some dim upper abode, and prostrate themselves in worship. All was as he had used it, the lounge beside the bed, a huge water jar in one corner, a few religious pictures on the walls and nothing more. Outside the heavy rain of June fell steadily, and below the terrace the Ganges moaned and hastened on. I have seen it in other moods—seen it when the oleanders nodded and whispered to the roses on the terrace, when the great mango groves behind were full of blossoms, and the clang of the bells for evening worship broke the silence to make the place like a smile at time of prayer. And I have seen it in the terror of an Indian noon, full of coolness and flower fragrance. But never did it look so poor as that June night, and never was poverty made so beautiful.

Here great scholars and potentates have been proud to be received—"And they seemed," said one who was often present, "like children before our Lord!"

He, at least knew nothing of the difference made by wealth and learning in the world. He dismissed the most important man of his district with a frown from his presence because he stood upon his riches and his name; he would leave companies of distinguished persons to themselves; and he would spend hours listening to the confidences of an anxious woman about her home, or in the instruction of some nameless lad. Yet his touch fell on none lightly. A great preacher, known to the West as to the East, changed his teaching when he knew him, in this new thought of the Motherhood of God. And many of the strongest men in India to-day, sat at his feet in their boyhood. An unlettered peasant, from the Brahmins of the villages, scarcely able to read and write he seemed, yet if original thought and wide reading are enough, he was a profound scholar. For he had a remarkable ear and memory that made him retain the sounds of the Sanskrit perfectly, with the translation, and as a vast quantity of literature was read and recited to him from time to time, he had acquired in this way an uncommonly large store.

In those years of which we are now speaking, the last twenty of his life, he was a great light, known as a saint throughout Bengal, the North-West Provinces and Nepal, and much visited, in the informal Eastern way. Men felt themselves in his presence to be dealing with forces that they could not guage, drawing on wisdom which they were unable to fathom. As if he were great music, they touched there the state that mighty music hints at, and went away saner, sweeter, stronger to their daily tasks.

Yet all this time his real inner life was lived amongst that group of young men who had foresworn the common motives of existence, to call themselves his disciples. He was rarely without one or two in immediate attendance, and many were with him day and night for weeks and months together.

Some were mere boys, and it was fitting that laughter and frolic should make a large part of the life together. Their Master was never sad. A gentle gaiety seemed the very air he breathed, broken indeed by the constant trance of rapture, and by the wonderful inspiration of his mood afterwards. "When it is night to all beings, then is the man of self-control awake: when all beings are awake, then is the night of the man of knowledge," he would chant, waking them during the dark hours to come out and meditate in the starlight, while many a day was spent swinging on the elephant creeper that his own hands had planted, amidst laughter and picnicking in the garden. The stream of days flowed on, without apparent plan or purpose,—yet all unnoticed a few leading ideas were being insisted on; a story here and there was building up the knowledge of that tremendous struggle through which he had attained to peace; they were watching him deal with men and things: above all, they were bathing in that Ocean of the Real to which his presence was a perpetual access.

And is not this the wisest of all teaching, to make sure of essentials, and leave the minds of the instructed to work out their own results, like the young plant growing up from seed? For we may be sure of one thing,—the order that is imposed upon us may become geometrical, but only the order that we create ourselves can become organic. It was the old Indian ideal of a university, to live in the forest with the Master and realise the meaning of culture in the touch of his personality.

These men to whom Ramakrishna Paramahamsa entrusted the mission and teaching of his "Divine Mother"—for he never dreamt of them as his own,—were chiefly graduates from the neighbouring colleges, many of them deeply tinged with the Western reaction which was the temper of that day. The distance between them and Christianity was shorter than would now seem possible. They were touched by its evidence of purity and enthusiasm for humanity, and full of a very genuine love for the New Testament. Occidental influences had stirred them to ideas of patriotism otherwise foreign to the Hindu temperament. They were looking for great things from the adoption of a more European taste and style of living. Above all, they had conceived the idea that India was being ruined by idolatry, and that the one thing incumbent on them was to do what in them lay, to sweep away every image and relic of degraded superstition, and to work for her emancipation from caste, from the zenana system, and from whatever else had till now been considered her distinctive institutions.

Speaking broadly, many of the finest minds of the Indian universities of that time felt thus, and these young disciples of Ramakrishna were among their following.

Suddenly they found themselves face to face with this ascetic saint of the old orthodox Hindu pattern. Gentle, without solemnity or affectation, full of humour, living in his garden almost nude, knowing little of the English save on hearsay, as a queer folk from overseas, the old man held them by a spell they could neither analyse nor break.

His perfect sincerity and gigantic purity made themselves felt even by youth, but against his intellect some made a desperate resistance. Long, long after, one of them said, "I was always looking for something that would prove him to be holy! It took me six years to understand that *he was not holy*, because he had become holiness itself!"

He was glad to hear all they could tell him of the Bible. Christianity was in the air in those days, and he had loved Christ and worshipped Him long before they came to him; but he bated no jot of his own devotion to Kali. "As sugar," he said, "is made into various figures of birds and beasts, so one sweet Mother Divine is worshipped in various climes and ages under various name and forms. Different creeds are but different paths to reach the Supreme."

The ritual of Kali-worship is the only existing provision in India for animal sacrifice. This means something entirely different from the Jewish notion of propitiation. There is no idea whatever of making compensation for sin: the whole intention is to offer meat-food first to the Mother, for Her use and blessing. No meat is eaten by the the orthodox Hindu without being consecrated in this way, whether he be otherwise a Kali-worshipper or not. But the Anglicised portion of the community, while consuming vastly more animal food than their conservative brethren, take great exception to these preliminaries, and have perhaps concentrated on this particular creed in consequence, all the horror with which idolatry as a whole inspires them. These were the associations of the disciples with Her whom their Master called his "Divine Mother."

But it was not Kali only: there

was not a symbol in India that he had not worshipped and did not love; not a worshipper, by whatever rite, whose special need he had not felt in his own nature, and borne till it was satisfied; not a prayer, or ecstasy, or vision that he did not reverence and understand, giving it its true place in a growing knowledge.

His was in fact the most perfect religious culture that the mind can conceive. The doctrine that "different creeds are but different paths to reach God," propounded in a general way, was not new in India. But taught as this man taught it, with his strong contention that it was the actual duty of men to follow their own faith, for the world gained by many-centredness; with his intense conviction "in whatsoever name or form you desire to know God, in that very name and form you will see Him;" with his assurance that rites and ceremonies contain religious experience, as the husk contains the germ; and above all, with that love that said of every faith, "Bow down and adore where others kneel, for where so many have worshipped, the Lord will manifest Himself."—it was unique in the world's history.

To those who have learnt even a a little of the authenticity of the religious consciousness, it is not difficult to see intellectually that creeds may bear to each other the relation of contemporary languages, all expressive of that one consciousness. But Ramakrishna in the garden of the Kali-temple, was a direct embodiment of the impulse to speak to each in his own language and tell him how to reach the goal. In this man's love there was no limitation anywhere. Let one be sincere, and neither race, nor history, nor stage of developement could cut him off. Each who came to him had his own place given to him, and kept it. His longing was for the salvation of every soul in a whole world. A universe from which one, most insignificant, was missing, could not have seemed perfect in his eyes.

Love such as this carries all hearts at last. Only such love deserves the name of God the Mother.

He was entirely abandoned to this great passion. There was nothing in him that remembered anything else. In the long years of self-discipline he had knelt to worship the very lowest, doing menial service for them with his own hands; in the last days of his life when he lay dying of cancer in the throat and speech was agony, he would insist on teaching all who came to him for help.

This was the secret that his disciples learnt by degrees. But on the outside, how free from display it was!

The old man sits chatting quietly with his boys. Now, with a twinkle of the eyes, he gives worldly advice to one—"Raise the hood (alluding to the cobra), but do not bite!" Again in a deeper moment, "There are thirty-six letter in the alphabet, and three of them, say 'suffer.'" (Bengali has three s's, which are so pronounced).

Everything taught its lesson, even the folklore of the district, and the quaint superstitions of the uneducated. In Ramakrishna's eyes, doubtless, much of human learning was on a level at bottom with the legend of the philosopher's stone ; but let a man see to it that he touched the feet of God, and whatever was his would become pure gold. Little incidents that occurred would all become the text of some remark, often of great profundity. Even a half-cooked vegetable would furnish a metaphor, it was like the aspirant who, falling short of perfection, is not yet all humility and tenderness. The bell, whose distinct strokes could be heard from the neighbouring temple die away into a long common vibration would remind him that God is both with form and without form too, and He is that which transcends form and formlessness.

There was wit too. All the saintliness in the world would not prevent a laugh at the man who was so indifferent to wordly interests that he permitted his wife to limit his charities.

And then, even as he talked with them, something would stir him deeper. A great light would come on his face, and he would pass, as they, awed, sat and watched, into the state of divine ecstasy, the inner vision of the Mother.

So, day by day, unutterable love and burning renunciation were woven into the texture of their lives, till one exclaimed, "It was not what he taught us, but that life that we lived with him! And that can never be told!"

At last came a summer night towards the time of full moon, when his disciples gathered round him, perceiving him to be passing into that beatitude from which there would be no return.

Even at that moment he rose suddenly to answer a thought in the mind of one. And then he left them, while one, whose music he had loved, chanted over him the name of God.

Later, in the dark, came a

woman, sitting at his feet crying softly, and calling him "Mother." It was that disciple who had been his wife.

During their after lives, when the boys had become men, and had begun to carry the message of their great Teacher far and near, they found that nothing he had given them was more precious than the story of his own early struggle and attainment. With the outer circumstances of his boyhood they were familiar, having mixed freely with his relatives and village neighbours, whenever these chose to visit Dukineshwar.

India is probably the one country in the world where a man can be awake to the meaning of his life from his infancy without having a whole growth of superstitions become heart of his heart at the same time. No doubt superstition is there, but it is possible for it to drop away imperceptibly as, to use Ramakrishna's own expression, the dried petals drop from the ripening fruit.

In this sense he seems to have been awake from the beginning. He had inherited the long-garnered knowledge of his race, that religion is no matter of belief but of experience. The worship of the Great God of Getting-on disgusted him ; and he longed to attain the sweetness of Divine Union even in boyhood. With all this, he kept caste strictly, and without thought of personal comfort.

At twenty years of age, however, all these elements became absorbed in one supreme desire. Pressure of many circumstances had assigned to him the duty of acting as assistant priest in the Kali-temple at Dukineshwar. We must think how it would work on a strongly religious temperament to find itself set apart for the service of God. We must remember also that the utterances of Ram Prasad and many another devotee of Kali were part of the common language of the country. It was as if his chosen way were pointed out to him. It was only for him now to traverse it.

His duty was to swing lights and flowers before the image, in the beautiful arooti ceremony.

But his whole nature had gone down in passionate yearning for the Mother Herself. One question, "Is this real? Is this real?" rang eternally in his ears. And he could not perform even this simple task efficiently. Sometimes he would swing the lights all day, sometimes he would forget them altogether, lost in a maze of agonised supplication.

The tale went about that he was mad, and as, everywhere, people will try by a dose of this world to drive out the other, his relations decided that the distraction of a wedding would give him his only chance of a cure. It was in this way that he was married to a little girl who long afterwards came to him and became one of the greatest of his disciples.

But a wedding-feast proved no mitigation of a struggle so tremendous, so overwhelmingly actual, and he had to be released from his stint of work. No doubt he would have been dismissed also from the garden but that the owners of the temple had recognised his genius and protected him.

The associations of this new period cluster thick round a great banyan-tree, and a wooden hut that once stood near it. The tree stands in the wilder part of the garden, close to the river, in perfect seclusion. Five stems grow together, and round the entwined trunk is built a terraced seat of brickwork. At the north-western corner a great bough of the Bo species has grown down across the bench, and tradition says that this covers the exact spot in which realisation was achieved. Be this as it may, the place was the scene of continuous meditation and austerity for many years. Not that the asceticism seems to have been pre-meditated. It would appear rather to have been the inevitable result of something deeper. Ramakrishna did not forbid himself to sleep or eat, he was unable to do either. He did not force himself to neglect his person, he entirely forgot it.

Driven on by his own nature, impelled from within by that irresistible necessity that had called him into being, without one rest or relaxation, for twelve long years at least, he persisted in that inner warfare. Then, at last, the goal was attained. The Mother revealed Herself. From that moment his personality was that of a little child, satisfied that he was in Her arms.

. . . . .

He had discovered a great secret, when he would break a disposition, he would reduce it to a concrete instance, and battle with it there. It was so that he had night after night performed that act of cleansing that was to rid him of social pride.

Now as he came slowly back to life out of the rapture of Eternal Union, having perceived the whole of Nature as himself, he yet, with his quickened senses, saw many elements in human life for which he had not actually traced the path.

And so, one by one, he took these as questions on the simplest plane. Beginning with that worship of Krishna which is related to his own as the Catholic Church to the Protestant, he made himself in all ways one with it. He ate and dressed and talked like the lovers of Hari,—and he ended by identifying devotion to Krishna with the love of Kali. So it was with Mohammedanism, and so with Christianity. Amongst his race, the Musselman is abhorred, and the dead are regarded as unclean. Yet he lived in a Mohammedan burial-ground till his end was achieved. It was not he who did these things. It was that Great Love that he felt within and called his Mother. He was not humble, but he seemed to have forgotten that Ramakrishna had ever been.

Then came the strangest phase of all. He would realise God as a woman! It was the flowering point of a certain tender chivalry that had always marked him, and makes his life the true emancipation of Indian women. His method, here and always, was the same,—to forget his own past and cause it to be forgotten. So he made every detail of their lives his own, and went to visit his wife in her village home, that he might find his friends entirely amongst her acquaintances and share every joy and sorrow of their hearts. Till at last he satisfied himself that the secret victory could also be attained in the straight path of womanhood.

And herein surely lies the gist of his life. As a mother's love justifies the existence of *all* her children, however unsympathetically they be judged by others, so he, the embodiment of the World-Mother, would take up whole areas of living and assert the place of each in the complete harmony of life.

And is it not a great doctrine,—that every man's cottage-door stands open on some high-road to the Infinite? Is it not immeasurably consoling, this cry of "No more idolatry! No more condemnation!" but to every man where he stands, using the means that lies to his hand—"Fix thine heart upon the Lord thy God, and let thine eyes look right on!"

It was as a seal upon this teaching that whoever came to Ramakrishna afterwards went away with profound courage. For the Master put his finger always upon the core of strength, and even his limitations became as wings upon the feet to the man so touched.

So with social customs and public movements, he destroyed no institutions: he did everything to make men and women strong in them. His friendship was given unhesitatingly to the leaders of reforming sects, and as readily to the despised artists of the theatre, while at the same time he was worshipped by the orthodox.

And yet he appeared quite unconscious of what he did. He seemed to act on divine instinct, like a child, and like a child, to be always superbly right. He was content to live, and leave to others to explain. Long ago, in early manhood, it had been no desire to become a teacher, but the longing to find the Real, that had driven him forth on the supreme quest. Now, it was because he would satisfy his unspeakable yearning over men and women that he tried every path to find God. Had one been left untrodden, his own soul would have gone seeking still. He never became the director of any, for in after life, it is said, he could not even imagine himself a teacher. He scattered his knowledge broadcast, and each took what he would.

We learn in him that greatness, and harmony, and beauty are all results. Our concern is not with them, but with those more elemental matters of simplicity and sincerity and whole-hearted devotion that lie close to us.

He is a witness to the world that the old Indian wisdom was not in vain. It is of course true that in no other country could he have occurred. But it is not true that he expresses the mind of India alone, or even chiefly. For in him meet the feeling and thought of all mankind, and he, Ramakrishna, the devotee of Kali, represents *Humanity*.

The Voice of the Mother.

ARISE, My child, and go forth a man! Bear manfully what is thy lot to bear; that which comes to thy hand to be done, do with full strength and fear not. Forget not that I, the giver of manhood, the giver of womanhood, the holder of victory, am thy Mother.

Think not life is serious! What is destiny but thy Mother's play? Come, be My playfellow awhile,—meet all happenings merrily.

Murmurest thou of need of purpose? Think'st thou the ball is purposeless, with which the Mother plays? Know'st thou not that Her toy is a thunderbolt, charged with power to shatter the worlds, at the turn of Her wrist? Ask not of plans. Needs the arrow any plan when it is loosed from the bow? Such art thou. When the life is lived, the plan will stand revealed. Till then, O child of time, know nothing!

My sport is unerring. For that alone set forth on the day's journey. Think it was for *My* pleasure thou camest forth into the world, and for that again, when night falls, and My desire is accomplished, I shall withdraw thee to My rest. Ask nothing. See nothing. Plan nothing. Let My will flow through thee, as the ocean through an empty shell.

But this thing understand. Not one movement shall be in vain. Not one effort shall fail at last. The dream shall be less, not greater, than the deed. Thou shalt go here or there for some petty reason, and thy going shall subserve great ends. Thou shalt meet and speak with many, but some few shall be Mine from the beginning. With these thou shall exchange a secret sign, and they shall follow with thee.

And that sign ?

Deep in the heart of hearts of Mine own flashes the sacrificial knife of Kali. Worshippers of the Mother are they from their birth in Her incarnation of the sword.

Lovers of death are they,—not lovers of life—and of storm and stress.

Such shall come to thee with torch unlit for fire. My voice cries out over the teeming earth for lives, for the lives and blood of the crowned kings of men. Remember that I Who cry have shown also the way to answer. For of every kind has the mother been the first, for proection of her flock, to leap to death.

Religion, called by whatever name, has been ever the love of death. But to-day the flame of renunciation shall be lighted in My lands and consume men with a psssion beyond control of thought. Then shall My people thirst for self-sacrifice as others for enjoyment. Then shall labour and suffering and service be counted sweet instead of bitter. For this age is great in time, and I, even I, Kali, am the Mother of the nations.

Shrink not from defeat, embrace despair. Pain is not different from pleasure, if I will both. Rejoice therefore, when thou comest to the place of tears, and see Me smile. At such spots do I keep My tryst with men, and fold them deep into My heart.

Uproot every interest that would conflict with Mine. Neither love, nor friendship, nor comfort, nor home, may make its voice heard when I speak. Pass from a palace to plunge into the ocean of terror, —from the chamber of ease to stand guard in a burning city. Know that as the one is unreal, so also is the other. Meet fate with a smile.

Look for no mercy for thyself, and I shall make thee bearer of great vessels of mercy to others. Accept bravely thine own darkness and thy lamp shall cheer many. Fulfil gladly the meanest service, and leave high places unsought.

Be steadfast in the toil I set thee. Weave well the warp into the woof. Shrink from no demand that the task makes on thee. Feel no responsibility. Ask for no reward.

Strong, fearless, resolute,—when the sun sets, and the game is done, thou shalt know well, little one, that I, Kali, the giver of manhood, the giver of womanhood, and the withholder of victory, am thy Mother.

A Visit to Dukineshwar.

"Thou wilt keep him in perfect peace, whose mind is stayed on Thee."—*Isaiah*,

HE was not in the vastness. And the Soul, lying on a housetop on the Earth, and ooking forth into the uttermost of space, realised the solitude and trembled.

Then came one whose voice spake within the heart, saying very gently, "Come thou away into that quiet place and rest awhile. There it may be that thou shalt speak with Him." And that soul arose, following after, as it were, the Angel of the Presence,—who bore white lilies, and about his feet played flames, and his eyes to look into were like mighty waters—and came by many ways unto the Lord's own garden, and rested there.

And there was in that garden a place where five trees grew together, beneath which oftentimes had the Master sat and prayed and entered into glory. Thither went the soul, laden with sorrowful queries and needs, and being received into the silence, waited.

On the left flowed the river, and the great barges went past swiftly, with sails full set. Beneath, the dead leaves stirred in the breeze, or rustled under the footsteps of a mouse. And on the branches above fell the flood of moonlight, dropping through and making spaces on the brickwork, all outlined by quivering leaves and moving stems.

The whispers of river and trees and lone night-creatures were the only sounds that could be heard.

. . . . .

"Those with whom I was wont to come, O Master, are absent now. In far distant and separate lands think they upon this place. I would make memorial for them at Thy feet to-night!"

And the Lord said—"It is well. My own are ever Mine. I bear their burdens; I guide their footsteps; and at last I bring them to that haven where they would be. There are three here to-night, My child, not one. Be assured."

"Some whom we love, O Lord, are in fetters of suffering. With hearts cramped by fear they look out upon their world. One longs for death because life is bitter: to others, life comes so hard that we almost ask for death for them. We pray Thee, give these ease, or that light that makes ease of no account."

And the Lord, smiling, listened—

"It cannot be, O Lord, that for the People we can do nothing! In the midst of terrible calamity, shrinking from the gaze of death, or striving against the blow that will rob them of the beloved: sleeping hard in the air of poisonous swamps, ill-fed, ignorant, and oppressed, it cannot be that we, so much more fortunate, can share *nothing* with them. It cannot be that Thou wilt tell us it is vain to struggle.

"And what would you have?"

"Only the right to share their danger, if nothing can be done. Only to hold their hands and hearten them—to perform some menial service for them—not to feel utterly cut off from fellowship, while they tread the winepress of despair!"

"Is this all?"

"Nay, if it were granted to us to serve truly—that would be blessedness. If we might indeed bring help, then the cup were full. But even without this we pray to be allowed the freedom where men do what they can, without thought o self. Command us not forever to think of the necessities of life. Grant us to give, and leave with Thee, and remember not whether life or death we shall take away."

And there was long silence. And at last the Voice, very gentle and reproachful—

"O foolish Children! Have ye yet to learn that this love that speaks in your hearts is not yours but Mine? Must ye struggle and plead with me for My own? Know ye not that difficulties and discouragements but point out the way in which I would guide you? Strive on and fear not! That way shall be found! Can *My* love be baffled? . . . Is yours more than its feeblest utterance? Remember

—'Thy right is only to action : thy right is never to the fruit thereof.' Maybe this struggle is itself your action. Yours not to ask how it shall end . . . . Your love is not separate from Mine. Know that these two are one . . . ."

And as the words died away, those souls rested for a moment in the sight of a Universe that was all Mother—of a love of which the love of human mothers for their children is but a feeble glimmer—of a life that whether hard or happy-seeming, was all alike the dealing of that Universe-Mother with Her babes.

. . . .

And the Master put forth His hand in that place and blessed His worshippers.

An Intercession.

"These are the days that must happen to
you:
You shall not heap up what is called
riches.
You shall scatter with lavish hand all that
you earn or achieve.
You but arrive at the city to which you are
destined,
You hardly settle yourself to satisfaction,
before you are called, by an irresistible
call, to depart.
You shall be treated to the ironical smiles
and mockings of those who remain
behind you.
What beckonings of love you receive you
shall answer with passionate kisses of
parting.
You shall not allow the hold of those who
spread their reached hands towards
you."

Walt Whitman.

MOTHER! Far away, one whom I love is very sad to-day. His heart calls to mine for help, but though I tell him how I love him, I leave him still uncheered. How is it? I know he thinks towards me, I know I talk with him. Yet I long to see him, and hear him, and comfort him face to face!

My child, if this were not so, the sense-life would not be yours, or would not hold you. When you have reached that place where the communion of souls is enough, you will find that it is *more* than the knowledge of the senses, faith will already be swallowed up in sight.

But, oh Mother, what can I now do to ease this craving pain? I prayed for the vision of Râghunath*

*The vision of Râghunath is one of the eight perfections. It consists in feeling the sufferings of others as if they were our own. Many stories of the saints, especially those of the stigmata, give us special cases of it. It is told of a Hindu devotee, that when a bullock was smitten cruelly in his presence he screamed and fell down

and did not know that it meant torture multiplied a thousand fold. When one is in trouble oneself, one's own little world lies in gloom ; outside, the busy feet pass up and down beneath the windows, the birds build nests, and the children play in the sunshine, as before : but the universe becomes all black when the beloved suffers.

Cease, My child, from inordinate affection. Give Me your heart, and let Me govern it alone. Be the *witness* of earth's joys and sorrows, sharing them not. Thus only can you keep yourself from entanglement, and attain to peace.

But peace for myself, dear Mother, why should I seek? How can I turn a deaf ear to his voice that calls me, adding another pang to the heartache of a life, and go away myself, and be at peace? Give *him*

fainting; and when the passers-by ran to his assistance, he was found to bear the marks of the lashes on his own back.

The allusion here is perhaps to one of the earlier steps in the acquirement of this perfection, when we have a deepened appreciation of the pain of those we love.

that inner peace! Let me win it for him, if Thou wilt be kind! But I cannot will to fail him in his need and loneliness, even to gain Thy blessing!

. . . . . .

Ah foolish one! Every thought of love that you send out to answer his, becomes a fetter of iron to hold him in life's anguish. Hide you yourself in My heart, My child, and he, too, will come home to Me. For your *love's* sake, let your voice cease to be one with the voices of the world. Let it come to him only in Mine, when that is borne on the south wind at the time of sunset, calling him gently to worship at My feet. Let it be one with transcendent love, with infinite freedom. Only thus can you satisfy him. Only by withdrawing yourself can you bring him peace.

. . . . . .

Mother! I yield. Take me, I pray Thee, into Thine own heart. Let me not look back. If Thou wilt call me I shall find my way there, surely, though my eyes now are blind with tears.

And for those I love, shall I trust Thy mercy less than I trust mine own?

Yet if at the last they seem to stumble, if the foot slip, or Thy voice fail them by the way, promise, dear Mother, once more to wake me from the dream of bliss. Cast me out from Thy heart, I beg of Thee, and let those who so need Thee, go in before to peace!

Silly, silly child! Like a helpless bird you beat your wings of littleness against My grace! Look up and laugh! For already the cloud that seemed so black is passing. Already the clasp of hands about the heart is loosened. *Two* souls draw the long breath of strength and relief. The feet of *two* who come to Me are shod with gladness. The hearts of two beat high, for the conquest born of renunciation.

The Story of Kali.

Written for Baby Legget, at Bally, Calcutta, Christmas 1898.

BABY DARLING, what is the very first thing you remember? Is it not lying on mother's lap, and looking up into her eyes, and laughing?

Did you ever play hide and seek with mother? Mother's eyes shut, and baby was not. She opened them, and there was baby! Then baby's eyes shut, and where was mother? But they opened again, and——oh!

When mother's eyes were shut, where was she? There all the time? But you could not see her eyes. Yet she was there.

Baby, some people think God is just like that. A great great Mother—so great that all this big world is Her baby. God is playing with Her world, and She shuts Her eyes. Then, all our lives long, baby darling, we try to catch the Great Mother peeping. And if any of us can do that, if any of us can look into the eyes of God, just once, just for a minute,—do you know what happens? . . . That person at once knows all secrets, and he becomes strong and wise and loving, and he never, never forgets that moment.

And when you win like that, when you catch the Mother looking, something else happens. Something lovely. All Her other children come and play with you. The little birds come, and the wee lambs love you, and the wild rabbits touch your feet, and the poor children in the streets, who are cold and hungry perhaps—poor children that the Great Mother loves most of all, because they seem to have no father or mother, and perhaps no home—poor children trust you, and make a place for you with them. We are all sitting on the Mother's lap, but these sit closest of all to Her breast.

And what do we call the Mother with Her eyes shut? We call her Kali.

. . . . . .

Were you ever for a very few minutes, unhappy? And did mother, or nurse, or auntie, or someone else, come and pick you up, and love you, and kiss you, till you were not unhappy any more?

Sometimes God is like that too. We get so frightened because those eyes will not open. We want to stop the game. We don't like it. We feel alone, and far away and lost. Then we cry out. It has grown quite dark, and still the Mother's eyes are shut. Let us play no longer. So we feel sometimes.

But the eyes are not shut, really. We think so, because it is dark all round. Just at that moment when you cried out, the beautiful eyes of the Mother opened and looked at Her child like two deep wells of love. And you, if you had seen, would have stopped playing all at once, and saying "Kali! Kali!" you would have hidden your little face on the Mother's shoulder, and listened to the beating of her heart instead!

And so, wee one, will you remember that the Great Mother Kali is everywhere? Even when the seems to be far away, it is only that you cannot see Her eyes. *This* mother goes away, and you cannot see her. But Kali is always there, always loving, and always ready to play with Her child.

And will you sometimes remember to stop playing, just for a minute, and to fold your little hands, and say, "Dear Mother Kali, let me see Your eyes!"

. . . .

There is another game of hide-and-seek that the Great Mother plays. This is more like a fairy story. She hides sometimes in other people. She hides in anything. Any day you might see Her eyes, just looking into mother's, or playing with a kitten, or picking up a bird that had fallen from its nest. Under all these forms you may find God playing at hide-and-seek!

When there is something to do for someone—Kali is calling us to play. We love that play. She Herself said once (She was hiding in someone, and He said it for Her).

"Inasmuch as ye did it unto one of the least of these, My little ones, ye did it unto Me." Is not that like a fairy story! And what funny places She, the Great Mother, can hide in! Another time She said "Lift the stone, and thou shalt find Me. Cleave the wood, and there am I!" Did you ever lift a stone or break a piece of wood to see what was inside? Did you ever think *that* was God—at the heart of things? How beautifully Kali plays! You might find Her *any*where!

. . . .

Does mother love baby when she is hiding from her? Why of course! else why should she hide? Even when her eyes are shut, is Mother loving baby? Why yes, see how she is laughing all the time!

And so with Kali. We need never be frightened, though Her eyes are long shut. She is laughing all the time. In Her own good time God will stop playing, and we shall look into Her eyes, and get away and away behind the world—straight "to the other end of nowhere," all at once.

So let us always run to play when we are called. Remember, little one, if any need anything you can give, your Mother is calling you to find Her! If anyone ask for something you can do, it is really Mother saying "Peep childie!" or when a new person comes for you to love, Kali is saying "Here am I!"

. . . .

There is something else. You love mother and father and auntie and nurse, and—, and—. Of course you do. Besides, they love you, and they are all so good and kind.

But far far away, mother has a brother, a big brother, like Holl. Do you love him too? Why? You never saw him. He never played with you.

No, but mother loves him. And you love all the people mother loves—don't you dearie? And so we love all the people Kali loves. *All* the children She plays with, and the lambs, and the flowers, and the great trees, and the little fishes. She loves all these, and She loves too the stars in the sky. And so do we. For we are Her children, and everything that She loves we love too, because She is the Mother, and we cannot help it.

Kali the Mother.

The stars are blotted out,
Clouds are covering clouds,
It is darkness, vibrant, sonant.
In the roaring whirling wind
Are the souls of a million lunatics,—
But loosed from the prison house,—
Wrenching trees by the roots,
Sweeping all from the path.
The sea has joined the fray,
And swirls up mountain-waves,
To reach the pitchy sky.
    Scattering plagues and sorrows,
    Dancing mad with joy,
    Come, Mother, Come!

For Terror is thy name,
Death is in Thy breath.
And every shaking step
Destroys a world for e'er.
Thou "Time" the All-Destroyer!
    Then come, O Mother, Come!

Who can misery love,
Dance in destruction's dance,
And hug the form of Death,—
    To him the Mother comes.

V.